Strange Game
in a Strange Land

Damian Balassone

A Poetic Celebration
of Australian Rules Football

WP

Published by:
Wilkinson Publishing Pty Ltd
ACN 006 042 173
Level 4, 2 Collins St Melbourne,
Victoria, Australia 3000
Ph: +61 3 9654 5446
www.wilkinsonpublishing.com.au

Cover art by Chris Rees (reesdesign.com.au).
Design Lee Walker.

A catalogue record for this
book is available from the
National Library of Australia

Planned date of publication: 11-2019
Title: Strange Game in a Strange Land
ISBN(s): 9781925927092 : Printed - Paperback.
Printed and bound in Australia by Griffin Press, part of Ovato

66

'To paint a picture so powerfully in so few lines
is an art not to be underestimated.
As a fellow poet, Balassone's class
and cleverness in eloquently carving out
his story is inspiring.'

RUPERT MCCALL

'A fabulator whose poetry is a sports field
of the four pillars in different ways:
Tribal, Home Ground Advantage,
Civility and Aesthetics.'

TED HOPKINS

'A virtuoso.'

LES MURRAY

Contents

Foreword

A few years ago, I was contacted by a keen young writer, about a narrative poem he was working on and hoping to publish. That was Damian Balassone and the poem was *Daniel Yammacoona*. He also sent me some quirky quatrains and couplets and other short football poems. They were published at www.footyalmanac.com.au, a website which appears to be a footy site but, when stripped back, is ultimately a writing site. Like all young writers – indeed, like all writers – he was playing with words and ideas.

It didn't take long for me to form the view that he had something to say, and that he would find a way of saying it, most likely in poetic form. He was interested in all those things which are meaningful to him: his family, his heritage, his suburban upbringing, popular culture, footy and the stuff of Australian life and more.

He wrote witty, clever, insightful short poems about his nonna's attitude to footy, Don Scott's dimple and half-back flankers, among many others. These short poems form a large part of this book.

This collection also contains two fine pieces of prose: an introductory essay about Damian and his interest in writing, and a beautiful tribute to his late father Don who died in 2015. In these pieces Damian, however reticently, invites us into his life in a way which confirms my suspicions were right: he does have something to say. Here's a writer whose first hero was Peter Daicos, and why not! What a footballer! As his natural curiosity, and his search for understanding, took him beyond Victoria Park, he found Bob Dylan, Oscar Wilde and Lord Byron, among others. I'm not sure there is a pecking order although it's pretty hard to compete with such a creative artist as the No. 35 at Collingwood. Lord Byron is no Peter Daicos.

I was delighted when Damian invited me to tap out a few words to introduce this fine collection. Damian's work, which addresses many topics, has appeared in a growing number of publications. Footy, and the meaning it contains, is at the heart of this book. He has lived footy, as have so many Australians. And so his words, based on his astute observation, and enthusiastic participation, are as true as a Peter Daicos torp.

John Harms

Introduction: Afternoon Shadows

In the early '80s the city of Melbourne is in the grip of footy fever. Carlton and Richmond are flying. Collingwood always in contention, providing hope for their legion of suffering fans. Essendon about to re-emerge as the Baby Bombers. Hawthorn in an unfamiliar trough that won't last long. Geelong perennial Preliminary Finalists awaiting their Messiah. Footy is everywhere. Scanlens footy cards. Huttons footy franks. Four'n Twenty pies. Mike Brady's soaring melodies. Record attendances. The Junior Supporters Club. Peter Landy and Seven's Big League. And then there are the names. The Flying Doormat. Lethal Leigh. Superboot. Schimma. The Flying Dutchman. The Macedonian Marvel.

Every Saturday Dad and I head off to watch the Pies. But we don't only venture to Victoria Park, we also travel deep into enemy territory to places such as Windy Hill, Princes Park, the Junction Oval, Moorabbin and the Western Oval. We even make the odd trip out to Kardinia Park. We always stand in the outer, the only exception being when the Pies play at the colossal venues VFL Park and the MCG where we are afforded the luxury of seating.

On Sundays it's up early and off to the footy clinic at Rieschiecks Reserve in East Doncaster, before dropping into my nonna's for lunch and a healthy dose of *World of Sport*. The school week consists of some classes sandwiched in between ferocious recess and lunchtime footy games. Upon returning home from school, I am out on the street in a matter of minutes booting the ball around until dark playing imaginary games, whilst commentating at the same time. In these seesawing battles the Pies always hit the lead in the dying seconds. The winning goal invariably coinciding with mum calling me in for dinner.

Imaginary games, Doncaster East 1982.
That's our house in the background.

Initially other kids in the street are involved in these games, but one by one they drop off. Some move houses. Increasing homework commitments claim others. While others simply do not possess the passion that I have for the game. This does not deter me. Friends or no friends, I will be out there until dark lost in these drop punt dreams. I don't realise it at the time, but not only am I developing my ball skills, but I am also cultivating my imagination. I can complete an entire round of footy in just one afternoon, with some after game semantics from Harry Beitzel and Tommy Lahiff thrown in for good measure. The neighbours wonder about the sanity of this kid who talks to himself while booting a ball around until dark.

Because various trees and lampposts at opposite ends of the court constitute the goals, there are two gardens in particular that cop a fair bit of unwanted attention from my exploits. Needless to say I am not popular in that street. But somehow I escape any form of serious punishment. I do cop a few sprays from grumpy old men every now and then, but I always manage to get my ball back. The only pain that is ever inflicted on me is from a Chihuahua that objects to me climbing the fence to retrieve my footy. The little mutt manages to take a chunk out of my leg, but I consider the confrontation a victory because I manage to get my ball back without having to ask the grumpy neighbour for permission to enter his backyard.

Then in 1983 the most wonderful thing happens. My little brother Chris is born. Soon I will have a mate to join me in these games. Preparations

With my little brother Chris in 1984.

are made early for his entry into the big time. We purchase a soft fluffy footy from the souvenir shop in the Collingwood Social Club and get to work. By the age of two he is holding his own in some classic one-on-one games in the family lounge room. Mum's teapot collection cops a hammering. His skills develop rapidly. He is a trusty left footer. These games will continue for years.

I go on to play footy for local clubs Doncaster Heights and Beverly Hills, as well as representing my schools Donvale Christian College and Doncaster High. I am a speedy rover/small forward who loves to have a bounce. Indeed the highlight of my career is having a bounce on the outer wing at Windy Hill during a Sun Shield game. I also have the honour of captaining my school on one occasion.

By the end of the '80s I am a skinny, mullet-haired kid with a chronic asthma condition, who is easily knocked off the ball. I can still get a kick, but it takes me a week to recover from a game, let alone front up for midweek training. I am at the end of the road. My footy dream is over. But an unexpected and joyous Collingwood premiership alleviates any pain associated with my failed footy ambitions. Over the preceding decade Dad and I had attended hundreds of Collingwood matches, so this premiership is cherished. In particular, we derive immense joy from studying the movements of the great football artist Peter Daicos.

I still love the game and Peter Daicos is my idol. But other heroes start to emerge. At first they are cinematic and appeal to the imagination of this delusional teenager; Rocky Balboa with his back to the wall; the Macho Man Randy Savage delivering his flying elbow from the top rope; Burt Lancaster entrancing the crowds in *The Rainmaker*. Lancaster's eloquence in the face of hostility makes a deep impression on me. Then the new decade heralds the entry of Bob Dylan into my life. Within 18 months I have worn out 30-odd Dylan albums and have ostracised most of my family in the process. I am then drawn to the epigrams of Oscar Wilde, the wit of Warren Zevon and the rhymes of Lord Byron. I especially like how the concluding couplets to Byron's ottava rima stanzas can equate to punchy stand-alone epigrams. You can say so much in so few words.

To me artists like Dylan, Lancaster and Wilde are no different to Peter Daicos. I am drawn to their brilliance just as I am drawn to the brilliance of Peter Matera bouncing the ball at high speed, or the exquisite skills of Darren Jarman, or the left foot of Jason Akermanis. It is all art to me. For me composing a witty couplet can be like having a bounce on the outer wing at Windy Hill; completing a pithy quatrain can be like extracting the ball from the pack and releasing a teammate into space with a pinpoint handball.

And so with that sentiment in mind, here is a selection of my footy-themed writings. The majority of the book is a sequence of short poems that attempt to capture the essence of Australian rules football in just a few lines (with a brief foray into some off-field activity and summer sports). The final piece *The Black and White Song and Dance* is a memoir about my father and my first game.

The First Game of the Season

A wife in marvellous Melbourne
may well be tried for treason
if she tries to stop her man attend
the first game of the season.

Strange Game in a Strange Land

While conquered nations play the games
their captors make them play,
'Let us play a *different* game,'
those quaint Australians say.

And watch them play their *different* game
on quagmire, grass and sand,
from orchards of the Apple Isle
to cliffs of Arnhem Land.

Marquee Player

On the field he plays it hard—
a ruthless Genghis Khan,
but off it he aspires to be
a dashing Don Juan.

Advice to a Young Footballer

'Don't worry what the papers say,
don't fear the words of men,
in Melbourne-town the footy boot
is mightier than the pen.'

Geelong Hymn #5

Sport is Barwon's medicine,
football is our tablet,
we don't care for Jesus Christ,
we have Gary Ablett.

My Nonna

When I started playing Aussie Rules,
my nonna's face turned red.
I asked her what the problem was,
and this is what she said:
'An oval ball, an oval ground,
for men with oval heads.'

The Transition

When a player's down on confidence,
when a forward's shooting blanks,
there is an ancient remedy:
it's called the Half-Back Flank.

Pre-match Address

The more he speaks, the more it seems,
his lines are all rehearsed,
and English is his second language—
Yeti is his first.

Richo Redeemed

And he can neither fathom, nor
believe the crowd's behaviour,
a week ago, they hated him,
but now he is a saviour.

The Vilified Player

If there's a cure for racism,
he cannot ascertain it,
but if he cannot change the world,
he'll have to entertain it.

King of Flings

After seasons of moonlighting
as a man about the town,
the king of flings was finally caught
with footy-shorts pulled down.

Sabbatical

Because you've been dehumanised by fame
you wanna go where no one knows your name.

Away Game in Perth

The players are surrounded by
a thousand hungry lions,
and in the sky the yellow sun
sizzles like an iron.

Moorcroft's Mark

If you blinked you would have missed it—
like the strike of a death adder—
he was soaring into outer space,
Johnson was his stepladder.

The King's Last Days

It seems like only yesterday
his grand career begun,
yet now he wanders Football Park,
the sperm of youth has swum.

Pilgrimage

A nervous kid runs up the race,
a million voices roar,
but when he treads the hallowed turf
his ancient spirit soars.

Tanami Pre-game

They've gathered in the scanty shade
to watch the big men fly.
The field looks like a wildlife park:
goannas amble by.

But when the players take the field
the crowd arise and cheer,
and in the blinking of an eye
goannas disappear.

The Night Footballer

When Gaz returns to Simonds stadium,
the moonlight dances on his cranium.

Outside the Ground

An overcrowded metro train
is nearing Richmond station,
the fabled Melbourne Cricket Ground
the common destination

where feisty boys in fluro smocks
patrol like feudal lords,
with gusto they repeat the word:
'Rec-ords! Rec-ords! Rec-ords!'

Don Scott's Dimple

When Scotty lifts the trophy up
his dimple mirrors on the cup.

Last Days of the Kid

The kid was once a champion
who thrilled the colosseum,
but now he is an artefact
inside a freak museum.

Adam Goodes vs. Daniel Wells

When Goodsey played on Daniel Wells,
Who won out? 'Twas hard to tell.
The duel was close from where I stood:
Goodes played well and Wells played good.

Marvel

Though hard against the boundary line
he executes a dribble kick.
The footy skips across the turf,
then somehow trickles through the sticks.

Barassi and Blight

The angle's tight and Malcolm Blight
believes he'll make this work,
but even though he slots the goal...
Barassi goes berserk.

The Country Footballer

'I play the game because I love it—
not for hollow cheers,
but those who play for man's acclaim
are prisoners to their fears.'

Ovens Murray Footballer

I sat on the pine—
they did not rate me at Wodonga.
I asked for a trade...
and now I play for Yarrawonga.

The Rebound

We pepper the goals;
we kill ourselves trying to score.
Then we cough it up
and concede one out the backdoor.

Tackling Bontempelli

If I don't keep him quiet
the coach is a nutter,
but his arms are longer
than a broomstick putter
    and trying to pin this skinny wuss
    is like trying to tackle an octopus.

Lewis Melican

To label Melican
the ugly pelican
     is just not on,
because Melican
is not a pelican,
     he is a swan.

The Non-Drinker

His teammates are completely stunned,
they view with much suspicion
those pansies who do not partake
of anglicised traditions.

Magoos

What a dismal day it was!
The weather made him squirm:
grey skies, cold winds, incessant rain,
magpies plucking worms.

Daisy Pearce

The word is out at Casey Fields
that Melbourne's on a roll,
as Daisy pierces through the pack
and slots a crucial goal.

Sabrina

A posse of defenders
is unable to absorb
the awe-inspiring brilliance
of Sabrina Frederick-Traub.

Afternoon Shadows

The minute that he's home from school
he scampers down the hall
and slips into his trackie dacks
and grabs his treasured ball,

then yells to kids across the street;
they hear his fervent call,
and soon they gather round to play
the greatest game of all.

Retrieving the Footy from the Tree

I climb the neighbour's back veranda
and shake their precious jacaranda
until I hear the thrilling sound
of leather landing on the ground.

Opportunist

While others fly, he keeps his feet—
he knows his chance will come—
and when the Sherrin spills to ground
he gathers up the crumbs.

Gary Ablett Senior

When Gary Ablett
takes his tablets
that balding blonde bogan
resembles Hulk Hogan.

Robbie Flower at the Western Oval

The dazzling moves of Robbie Flower
evade these men of brutish power.
He baulks the wild men of the west,
then hits a teammate on the chest.

In autumn sun or winter shower
behold the skills of Robbie Flower,
but fans would give up everything
to watch him ply his trade in spring.

The Common Dominator

From seventy-nine to eighty-seven
the Baggers held four cups to heaven;
and the common denominator
was, of course, the Dominator.

Joy

The ball's in Leo Barry's hands.
The final siren sounds.
The sky is painted red and white...
and weeping joy abounds.

The Arm of Harmes

The arm
of Harmes
    that crosses the line
denies
the Pies
    in seventy-nine.

The Interceptor

McGovern soars above the pack
and thwarts another Pies attack.

Black and White Déjà vu

The siren sounds. The stands are filled
with joyous celebrations.
An old man is a child again
with shattered expectations.

He grabs his bag and flees the ground,
replaying way back when
he cried beneath September clouds.
He's eight years old again.

The Man from Moe

Craving interaction,
a lonely chap from Moe,
enters Young and Jackson
and has a pint with Chloe.

In Praise of Carbohydrates

It's well worth pointing out
that the night before a bout
   Rocky Mattioli
ate a bowl of ravioli.

Strange Dismissal

It sounds silly
but it's harsh
to be caught Lillee
bowled Marsh,
    but that's what happened to me
    the over prior to tea.

Strange Rain

Lightning strikes the picnic races.
Strange rain falls on sunburnt faces.
A horse stampedes against the storm.
A mob of grinning punters swarm
towards the bookies in the stands...
who cough up coin with jealous hands.

The Gambler at the Guillotine

The gambler racked up quite a debt,
but always claimed he'd pay it back.
They put a bounty on his head
and caught him at a country track.

They placed him in the guillotine,
then kindly granted one last wish.
He asked to hear the latest odds
and tipped the favourite in the fifth.

Sports Role Models

At first, I copied Baggio
and dwelt by Buddha's sacred pond.
But now I'm Joe DiMaggio
and chase a tall, curvaceous blonde.

Red Centre Bounce

All is now in readiness
upon that field of dust.
The umpy holds the ball aloft,
then slams it with a thrust.

It soars into the aqua sky,
the gangly ruckmen jump...
but when the leather hits the ground
the rovers cop the bumps.

The Dancing Footballer

He sharks it from the centre bounce—
a calculated theft—
and with the step of Fred Astaire
he swings onto his left.

Beach Footy

He scoops the Sherrin off the sand
and spins away from me,
then kicks a monstrous torp into
the Arafura Sea.

Tiwi Islands Grand Final

Imalu Tigers vs. Tuyu Buffaloes

The Tigers and the Buffaloes
are due to meet today.
Every woman, man and fly
have come to watch 'em play.

Their dazzling skills enthral the crowd;
they tap-dance with the ball,
and like a travelling carnival,
there is a part for all:

the seasoned star, the skinny kid,
the tall, the short, the dreamer,
the birdman flying through the air
to take a breathless screamer,

the loose man streaming down the wing,
the thrilling one-on-ones,
the goal sneak scouting by the packs
to gather up the crumbs.

St Kilda Parish Priest, 1966

Forgive me brethren if this sounds unkind:
but praise the lord for Barry Breen's behind.

On the Terrace

When gentiles slag Geelong's messiah,
the zealots speak in tongues of fire.

The Old Champ Re-signs

His brand new contract illustrated how
the golden calf was now the sacred cow.

Ode to Simon Prestigiacomo

The skills of Jarman are absurd,
and Aka on his non-preferred,
and Ross Glendinning in full flight,
and Barker reaching for the heights.

But let us not forget those men
who turn up time and time again
and duly sacrifice their game
to guard the best and biggest names.

Animal Enclosure

At Moorabbin, Derm and Spud go toe to toe,
and the larrikins are here to watch the show.

In the second quarter Frawley corners Derm
and rubs a lump of mud into his perm.

In the final term the Kid is out for blood
and cannons into Frawley with a thud,

as the two of them trade punches in the mud,
all the larrikins are barracking for Spud.

Footy Memorabilia

They say at Central District there's a box
that's fastened with at least a dozen locks.

It's kept behind a wall of tempered glass
and patrons must tread lightly when they pass.

It's rumoured that this deeply cherished box
contains a pair of Johnny Platten's jocks.

Flying Doormat

It seems that since the dawn of humankind
the bearded bald man punches from behind,
then tiptoes off his man without a trace
and somehow finds the ball with time and space.

Reappraising Praise

The roar of the rapturous crowd
enchanted me when I was young.

But what does it mean to be praised
if praise is from a fickle tongue?

Mongrel Punt Proverb

When scores are level in the last
and the final bell's about to blast

   and the greasy Sherrin lands
   into your trembling hands...

remember that a mongrel punt
is all it takes to hit the front.

Dasher

He works his way into the clear
with football in his palms,
and as he tears across the wing,
he tucks it under arm.

Sampi's Screamer

He seemed to stand upon their heads
the best part of a second,
but when a mere man scales the heights,
a tragic landing beckons...

yet somehow Ashley Sampi
landed softly on his feet,
and when he lined the big sticks up
he didn't miss a beat.

Debutant

Who is this wiry teenage kid,
this acrobatic dancer,
who dazzles like a butterfly
yet pounces like a panther?

Wimmera Centre Bounce

All is now in readiness
upon that field of thistles.
The maggot holds the ball aloft
then blows his screeching whistle.

Faith in the Antipodes

The Catholic has the Vatican,
the Jew, the synagogue,
the Buddhist has the temple,
the Aztec lauds the dog,

every culture looks towards
a supernatural force,
Australians have their footy fields...
oval shaped of course.

An Hour in Heaven

The demons dwell in heaven for an hour
when witnessing the skills of Robbie Flower.

The Half-Back Flankers

We strive to run the lines until
the opposition breaks.
Imagination is the name
we give to our mistakes.

After the Siren

When patrons leave the MCG
in buses, trams and trains,
the gulls descend from dizzy heights
and loot the lush terrain.

Song of the Seagull

Twilight-time, the MCG,
seagulls now are flying free,
as old men clean the littered stands,
the seagulls spy the fertile land.
The hordes have left in trams and trains,
only corporate men remain,
and while they sip their cold champagne
the seagulls sing in joyful strains:
'When you leave the footy ground,
we fly in from coastal towns.
What you have lost, we have found,
listen to our screeching sound!
Now don't complain, or ask us why;
this land is ours 'cos we can fly.
Possessing not a shred of skill
we feast until we've had our fill,
then once again we're homeward bound,
returning where the breakers pound.'

The Black and White Song and Dance

For Don Balassone 1943-2015

*The first VFL game I attended was Collingwood
versus Essendon at Victoria Park in 1980. I was seven.
Driving in from East Doncaster, Dad took the Eastern
Freeway before veering off at the Chandler Highway
exit. We then snaked our way through Yarra Boulevard,
before parking up at Yarra Falls and commencing a
long but enjoyable walk to the ground.*

*My reasons for becoming a Collingwood supporter
were quite trivial. A Jewish kid across the street who
I looked up to barracked for them and used to talk the
Pies up during our one-on-one street matches. But a
more likely reason was that my favourite TV show was
'The Incredible Hulk' starring Lou Ferringo. Due to
a striking resemblance to Ferringo, Rene Kink, one of
Collingwood's stars at the time, was nicknamed 'The
Incredible Hulk'. Whatever the reason, I was hooked
and became a black and white fanatic from a young age.*

*As we walked towards the ground, Dad was like a
tour guide pointing out all the local landmarks. He had
grown up here after migrating from Italy in 1950. I
soon discovered there was a strong family connection to
the area…*

Donato Balassone was born in 1943 in the Italian town of Sulmona in the Abruzzo region. Donato means donation and thus Donato has always marketed himself as a donation to mankind. Some have speculated that Balassone means 'song and dance man', so if we are to interpret his name literally, his singing and dancing have been a gift to the world. Sulmona is located at the foot of the Maiella massif and is perhaps best known as the birthplace of the poet Ovid, whose bronze statue stands in the town piazza. Donato's parents Alfonso and Concetta married in 1936. Their first son Pasquale was born in 1939. Not long after Donato was born in '43, Sulmona was subject to an American air raid. During the strike Concetta wrapped Donato in a blanket and ran for safety. When she finally found shelter she uncovered the blanket to find a blue-coloured baby, almost suffocated to death.

Sulmona is an ancient Roman town surrounded by farmland. Most of the families who lived there owned plots of land a few miles out of town. The Balassone's owned about five acres. Pasquale, who later became known as Peter, and Donato, who later became known as Don, helped out on the farm. Peter took the sheep to the mountains to eat grass, while Don assisted in digging crops – although being a small child meant he could wander off from time to time and pluck the luscious cherries from the trees. Don's first moment of self-awareness came while standing by a mountainside and being lit up by the Abruzzo sun. In an instant, he felt a oneness with the earth, universe and creation.

At about 10:30 each morning, the women arrived with baskets of food for a well-earned break. The diet consisted mainly of pasta, vegetables, corn, figs and cherries. Meat was a commodity they could not afford and the sheep they grazed were eventually sold for cash.

At this time there were numerous relatives living in the family household. Hence, there was limited space and resources to adequately cater for all. On top of that, Alfonso had two sisters who he felt were not chipping in. The last straw for Alfonso came when one of his sisters decided she wanted to become a nun. It was time to leave. He decided on Australia. There would be opportunities for the kids there.

Alfonso sailed for the antipodes in 1949. He would spend a year working and establishing himself in Melbourne before his wife and two sons would arrive. Later that year, Concetta, Peter and Don went to Rome to acquire the necessary paperwork for their immigration. One of Don's endearing memories of this trip is being surrounded by the grand beauty of St Peter's Square.

In early 1950 they boarded the ship *The Sorrento* from the Bay of Naples. As the ship departed, with the land of his birth slowly receding before his eyes, Don was filled with a sense of wonderment. For the next six weeks, Don and Peter roamed the ship barefoot while their mother Concetta was holed up in her cabin with severe seasickness. There were twenty or thirty friends from Sulmona on board, so the kids were treated like kings.

The imagery of the voyage was unforgettable: different coloured people in different coloured attire at African and Arabian ports, enormous barrels of bright-yellow bananas at Colombo, schools of dolphins following the ship, monstrous waves, migrating whales, flying fish leaping twenty feet into the air. But none of these sights were daunting to a little boy, but rather wondrous. This was the adventure of a lifetime.

As the ship approached Melbourne, six-year-old Don somehow spotted his father Alfonso amongst the massive crowd at the port. He had not seen him for a year. Alfonso had two ice-creams in his hands, which he miraculously managed to get to his sons through the portholes of the ship.

Soon after the family settled in Hotham Street, Collingwood. Alfonso was initially a labourer and later a storeman, while Concetta worked as a machinist in a shoe factory. Don vividly remembers his first day at school. A bully, sensing an easy target, was mouthing off at him. Though Don didn't understand a word of the tirade, he knew it wasn't nice and he thus proceeded to beat the daylights out of the bully. At St Joseph's Primary School he was a notorious fighter who never backed down, particularly from fights with bigger kids. His older brother Peter expressed his concerns to father Alfonso, who merely smiled.

The Balassone family, Collingwood in 1950.
Left to right: Peter, Concetta, Alfonso and Don.

Despite the propensity for fighting, Don maintains racism was never an issue for him. It may have been because he possessed blue eyes and fair skin, or perhaps because kids would no longer pick on him because they knew there'd be trouble. An incident that had a profound impact on him and won him over to the Aussie spirit occurred after his father was hit by a car and spent time in hospital with a broken leg. During this period Don recalls some strangers at the hospital befriending him, even though only years prior their respective countries had been at war. He was quickly drawn to the Aussie spirit, this ideal of mateship, the willingness to give someone a go, and sensed the positive implications of adopting such an attitude to others.

He was soon introduced to the Collingwood phenomenon. On Saturday afternoons he heard the roar of the crowd from the football stadium across the road. What was this strange game in a strange land? He was curious. Around this time he recalls an old man with a cap from across the street, looking down at him and telling him about the great Collingwood Football Club, the notable school friend was Graeme 'Jerker' Jenkin, best remembered as Alex Jesaulenko's stepladder in the 1970 Grand Final, but also a fine ruckman in his own right who went on to play over 100 games with the Pies.

Don excelled in sports at Collingwood Tech and became a school boy discus champion. Later that year he joined another great Collingwood institution, the Collingwood Harriers Athletics Club. During this period he trained and competed with Australian discus champions Ves Balodis and Harry Mitsilias, as well as sprinter Peter Norman, who later won a silver medal at the 1968 Olympics (famously sharing the dais with the 'Black Power Salute' medallists). Many years later Don returned to Collingwood Tech as a Maths and Science teacher before eventually becoming a Production Engineer and starting his own lighting and power business, lighting up the world with his torches.

After parking the car at Yarra Boulevard, we took the track past Dight Falls, where the salt water from the sea meets the fresh water of the Yarra River. Innumerable Magpies occupy the area and it is said that the Collingwood mascot was inspired by the magpies at Dights Falls. To a seven-year-old kid it seemed remarkable that such a tranquil place was located so close to the noise and chaos of the city. All the while, dad filled me in about his youth. All these stories strengthened my sense of attachment to the area. We then stepped out onto Studley Park Road. Slowly etching our way towards Mecca. We turned right onto Trenerry Crescent, before marching down Turner Street with the faithful. The black and white colours were everywhere. The exterior of the Rush Stand was adorned with black and white stripes. Stalls were selling scarves, flags, badges and posters. An old raggedy man was hawking peanuts. Scruffy kids were collecting aluminium cans. A large queue was gathered outside the Rush Stand gates. There was a strange inner-suburban smell in the air. Hot dogs, pies, chips, vinegar, jam doughnuts, beer, nicotine. Oh the excitement of passing through the turnstiles and into the stadium. We settled in the outer on the half-

forward flank as the Reserves were concluding. Had the game already started? Dad explained the concept of the Reserves to me. Thank God, I hadn't missed anything. The crowd continued to build. The Reserves trudged off. Suddenly a deafening roar pervaded the stadium and the banners were raised. It felt like the earth was shaking. Dad lifted me to his shoulders and I saw my black and white heroes emerge from the race of the Ryder Stand and burst through the banners.

Acknowledgements

Some of these poems have appeared previously, often in a slightly different form, in the following publications: *Back Page Lead, Blackmail Press (NZ), Daniel Yammacoona, Eureka Street, Light Poetry Magazine* (USA), *Lighten Up* (UK), *Long Bombs to Snake, News Weekly, Quadrant, Red Room Poetry: The Disappearing, The Footy Almanac, The Roar* and *The Women's Footy Almanac.* Thanks to the great John Harms and the mighty Footy Almanac community. Special thanks to my parents Don and Rosalia Balassone for their love and patience. And most of all, thanks to my wife Linda and our two beautiful daughters Alicia and Emma. Thanks for putting up with this dreamer.

About the Author

Damian Balassone's poems have appeared in
over 100 publications, most notably in *The New
York Times*. Described as a 'virtuoso' by legendary
Australian poet Les Murray, he is the author
of three volumes of poetry. His love of footy
stretches back to 1980 when he sat on his father's
shoulders in the outer of Victoria Park, studying the
movements of the Macedonian Marvel.